Royal Doulton

DESIGNING FINE CHINA

THE DESIGN PROCESS

Every piece of china is born in the imagination of the designer. A skilled artist is able to absorb many artistic traditions and trends, and create designs which are both practical and beautiful. Royal Doulton designers and modellers create every item that bears the famous backstamp – figures, Character Jugs, tableware, giftware and crystal. There are many stages through which a design must pass before it reaches the shop or department store. It can take up to a year for a figure or a piece of tableware to progress through the various stages from a modeller's desk and into production.

There are about 235 figures in the Royal Doulton figure range. They

BELOW: Modeller Alan Maslankowski with his creation 'The Charge of the Light Brigade' (HN 3718), a Prestige figure that was first issued in 1995.

include famous characters from history or literature, and figures created to express emotions or special events.

Some are new models from the talented Royal Doulton Studio; others are old favourites which were first modelled over 50 years ago. All have a quality which marks them as Doulton, and an HN number (after Harry Nixon) which places them in the record books.

MODELLING SCULPTURAL SUBJECTS

When an idea for a new model has been agreed with Royal Doulton's marketing and sales teams, the Art Director assigns the job to a skilled modeller. Many artists specialise in subjects or styles. The modeller produces a small clay figure known as a maquette to show the style of the proposed figure. Once the concept is agreed, a full-scale figure known as a 'clay' is created. The modeller uses research sketches and photographs as references to ensure that every detail of costume and expression is correct. After final approval, the model passes to the blocking and mould-making department. Here, the block-maker uses a sharp scalpel to cut the clay model into pieces from which individual moulds are made. Some complicated figures are cut into as many as 25 different pieces.

DESIGNING TABLEWARE

Nowhere can you see more clearly the importance of teamwork than in the creation of new Royal Doulton tableware. Skilled modellers produce the shape, which has to be both practical and aesthetically pleasing.

Surface designers create the pattern using pen, pencil or paint. Then, using special computer assisted design programmes, they transfer their drawings onto a screen where they can copy and repeat small sections of pattern in order to create a complete border. Finally, the pattern is tried on the many different items that make up a tableware service.

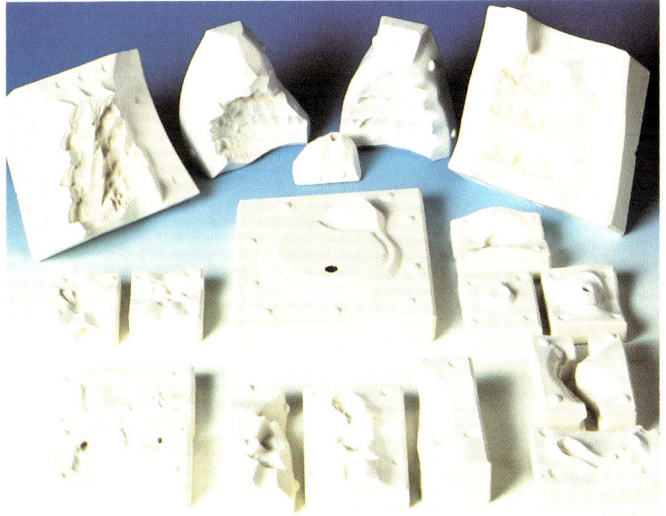

ABOVE: Several moulds are needed for just one figure.

BELOW: Designing tableware.

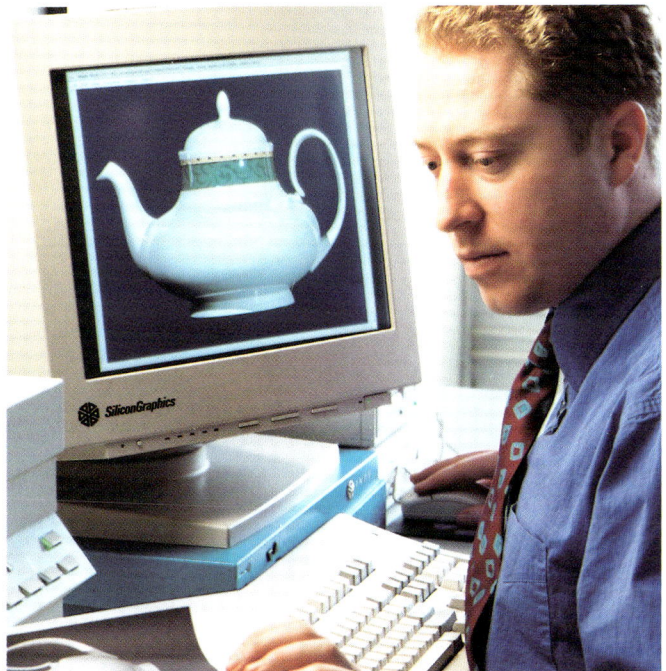

MAKING FINE CHINA

PREPARING CLAY BODIES

In many ways, making fine china is like baking a cake. The ingredients are mixed together, a shape is formed, it is baked in an oven and finally decorated. A mistake at any stage will spoil the finished piece, and every process involved calls for a great deal of experience and skill.

All china is made from a composition of china clay, Cornish stone, sand and hydroxyapatite. The Royal Doulton laboratory makes careful checks to maintain

high quality and consistency of the ingredients. The traditional method of mixing clay uses a massive machine known as a 'blunger'. The ingredients are individually mixed and then blended together with a precise amount of water in the blunger until a creamy liquid clay or 'slip' is produced.

The slip is sieved and pumped over powerful electromagnets to remove particles of iron which would appear as dark spots. The clay is pressed in a 'filter press' to remove excess water. The pressed 'cakes' of clay are fed into a 'pug mill' which kneads the clay. A vacuum pump removes air bubbles. If any air remains it will expand in the heat of the kiln and the china will explode.

ABOVE: Pouring slip (liquid clay) into a mould to cast a figure. After a period of drying, a skin of clay forms inside the mould. Excess slip is poured away and after more drying the moulds are opened.

ABOVE RIGHT: A figure assembler joins together the separate parts of a figure, using slip.

CASTING

Holloware shapes such as figures, teapots, coffee pots, cream jugs and vegetable dishes are made by the casting process using liquid clay or slip. The slip is poured into individual plaster-of-paris moulds that absorb the water from the slip until all the inner surfaces are lined with a coating of set clay. The slip has to remain in the moulds for a precisely controlled time to ensure that the cast pieces attain the correct thickness and strength. The moulds are opened up and the various pieces are removed.

ASSEMBLING

The soft clay parts are joined together with liquid slip to form the complete piece. The assembled figure or holloware shape is then 'fettled' so that any join or mould lines are smoothed away and left to dry. (After the first or 'biscuit' firing there is no trace of any joins.)

MAKING FLATWARE

Hand skills are very important in the creation of holloware shapes, but at Royal Doulton the most advanced tech-nology and machinery is used also to assist in the manufacture of tableware such as plates and saucers (known as flatware). Specialist items, such as large oval serving dishes, require the skills of an experienced dish-maker. The crafts-men who manipulate large pancakes of clay on a revolving wheel provide one of the highlights of the factory tour.

FLOWER-MAKING

Some figures hold a single flower, others a full bridal bouquet, and many of these minute flowers are individually made by hand by a small number of highly skilled women. Each flower is different, as are the figures' painted faces, so no two figures will ever be identical. To prevent the clay sticking to their fingers, the flower-makers keep their hands moist with olive oil, and to help shape each tiny petal they use fine tools, some no thicker than a sewing needle.

FIRING

The first firing is in a kiln where temperatures reach 1,250°C. The kilns today are electric, oil- or gas-fired, replacing the traditional picturesque bottle ovens. During this first, or 'biscuit', firing, the clay item will shrink by about 12.5% as water in the body evaporates.

GLAZING

The china is covered in 'glaze' or liquid glass. Figures are dipped by hand, but most tableware goes through an auto-matic glazing machine. Pieces undergo a second, or 'glost', firing, at around 1,050°C, before the sparkling white china moves to the decorating stage.

Some items, such as character figures and jugs, are decorated under the glaze. The colour decoration is applied to the biscuitware, and after drying it is glazed and then fired. The need for perfection guides the choice of production process.

BELOW: A flower-maker adds flowers to the figure 'Sarah' (HN 3380), using the same techniques introduced soon after the end of the Second World War.

LEFT: Dish-making using a plaster-of-paris mould to form the inside of the dish, and a profile tool to shape the outside. It requires many years of experience to produce oval dishes of an even thickness.

DECORATING

DECORATING FIGURES

Figures are decorated by hand, using a variety of techniques such as hand painting and fine sprays. The paints used are specially prepared ceramic pigments mixed with aniseed oil and diluted with turpentine or glycerine. The rich colours for which Royal Doulton is renowned are built up layer upon layer. For example, the red skirt of 'Top o' the Hill' (see front cover) is created with a layer of 'Massey's Orange', which is fired, over-painted with 'Harrison Pink', and fired again. The faces of figures are hand decorated by a few specialist artists. By the stroke of a fine sable brush, a figure can be laughing, coy or mysterious. Also within the decorating department is a select team who paint the Prestige and limited edition figures. These talented decorators will paint figures that take several months to create, often involving 20 or 30 colours.

DECORATING TABLEWARE

There are many ways of decorating tableware, but today most processes use a lithograph. The artist's original designs are photographically transferred onto a sheet of fine paper which is then coated with plastic. The lithographer applies the transfer with amazing dexterity. Each lithograph sheet is kept in a heated cupboard, soaked briefly in soapy water to loosen the transfer from the backing paper and then slid onto the china. Once in place, the lithograph is smoothed using a hand-held rubber 'squeegee' to remove air from under the transfer.

ABOVE: A Prestige figure painter decorates 'Jack Point'.

BELOW LEFT: A lithographer applies a transfer design.

BELOW: Hand gilding a jug.

Casual china, such as the Doulton Everyday range, is often produced by a newly developed direct printing method which transfers the artist's original design onto the ware by means of an engraved plate and a 'rubber bombe'. Some patterns are enhanced by borders of precious metal or colour. These can be added by machine or hand, depending on the delicacy of the work.

GILDING

Hand painted and gilded commissions are still a speciality at Royal Doulton. Artists in the company's Minton Fine Art Studio create individual works of art, using techniques that have been perfected over the past 100 years.

Raised paste gilding involves the building up of an intricate design by applying paste and then layers of 22-carat gold. One plate can take six days to decorate – and each costs £5,000.

FIRING

The third firing is in the decorating kiln, where the glaze softens to absorb the decoration. Once the ware is cooled, the

ABOVE LEFT: In the Visitor Centre, skilled hand painting can be admired.

patterns are permanently fixed in the glaze. Some figures and tableware designs are fired up to four times at the decorating stage, allowing artists to build up the colours and decoration needed to complete the designer's original vision.

ABOVE: The fine art of figure painting requires a very steady hand.

BELOW: Decorated figures are placed ready for firing in the kiln.

HISTORY OF ROYAL DOULTON

THE LAMBETH FACTORY

The name Doulton comes from the family who established the business in 1815. John Doulton's first pottery was on the banks of the Thames, in Lambeth, South London. Here he produced utilitarian saltglaze and stoneware pieces such as jars, bottles and flasks. The young Charles Dickens was employed by Warren's boot blacking makers to stick labels on Doulton stoneware jars and bottles. Five of John's sons joined him at the pottery. It was his second son, Henry, born in 1820, who joined the company as an apprentice, aged 15, and was the entrepreneur who diversified and expanded the company.

As well as establishing the world's first business to make stoneware drainpipes – an important contribution to social reforms at the time with the introduction of piped water and improved sanitation – Henry also encouraged and employed many students from the local Lambeth Art School. Among his protégés was the sculptor George Tinworth, whose modelling work included religious tableaux, favoured by Queen Victoria, as well as comical groups of mice and frogs.

In 1871, Hannah Barlow and her brother Arthur joined the newly established studio. Hannah's incised animal designs earned

her great merit, especially when John Ruskin bought one of her pots during a visit to the factory. Hannah was the first of many women artists to work at the Lambeth pottery. She was soon joined by her two sisters Lucy and Florence, all working in their own individual style. They were followed by countless others such as John Broad, Florence Lewis, Mark Marshall, Vera Huggins and Agnete Hoy, who continued to design art wares until the Lambeth factory closed in 1956.

BELOW: The last piece of pottery made at the Art Studios, Lambeth, before the factory closed in 1956.

BELOW: Two salt-glazed Doulton Ware humoresques by George Tinworth, c.1884–86.

RIGHT: A silver-rimmed Doulton Ware jug with incised decoration by Hannah Barlow.

THE FIRST ROYAL DOULTON CHINA

Having made his fortune in the production of stoneware and sanitaryware, Henry Doulton then decided to manufacture in Stoke-on-Trent. In 1877 he purchased the Pinder Bourne Company in Burslem – the site of the present Royal Doulton factory. A train missed by chance and a change of heart are the ingredients of a remarkable story behind the first Royal Doulton china, which was to have a far-reaching significance for the future of the company.

Art Director John Slater suggested to Henry Doulton that the company should begin to produce bone china. Henry agreed to allow Slater to experiment with producing and decorating bone china, but not to add a Doulton backstamp. On a visit to the factory, Henry Doulton discovered a porcelain dessert service in the warehouse carrying the Doulton mark. He was so enraged that he smashed dozens of pieces with his umbrella, sacked Slater and left for the railway station. Henry missed his train to London and stayed at the North Stafford Hotel overnight. The next morning he returned to the factory in a calmer frame of mind, sent for Slater, reinstated him and ordered him to 'call the architects' so that a china works could be built.

ABOVE: Artists in the Burslem Art Studio were renowned for their floral art wares. These are examples by David Dewsberry and Edward Raby.

BELOW: Hand painted and gilded tea cups and saucers, produced in the early 1900s at Burslem.

VOTES FOR WOMEN

Historically, ceramic objects have sometimes been used to make political statements, and several different pieces with a political message have been produced by Royal Doulton since the earliest years of its history in 1820. The inkwell depicting the Virago and inscribed 'Votes For Women' was modelled by Leslie Harradine in 1905 and produced in several different colours. The inkwell is now sought after by collectors and is one of the most admired pieces in the museum collection, bringing a smile to most visitors' faces – including that of Diana, Princess of Wales.

HISTORY OF ROYAL DOULTON

From 1884 onwards, Royal Doulton in Burslem produced the finest china with both lithographed and hand painted decoration. A studio of artists was developed, including Percy Curnock, David Dewsberry and Joseph Birbeck among others, who painted or gilded many beautiful designs. John Slater and chief modeller Charles Noke (later Art Director) created a range of distinctive shapes and decorative techniques. Many of these prestigious wares were shown at international exhibitions such as the World's Columbian Exposition in Chicago, USA, in 1893 where the company received seven gold medals.

Sir Henry Doulton died in 1897 and many may have felt that the company would fade without the great impetus of his energy and vision. This was not the case – his son Henry Lewis Doulton, combined with the creative talents of modeller Charles Noke, ensured that Royal Doulton not only survived but continued to expand. Noke became Art Director in 1914 and it was under him that many of the introductions now famous throughout the world were made: the innovative wares of the Burslem studio, including flambé and other experimental glazes; series wares; figures;

animal sculptures; and Character Jugs.

Successive Art Directors Jack Noke, Jo Ledger and Amanda Landi have continued to develop these collectors' ranges, adapting them to changing styles and fashions. They have continued to employ the best designers and modellers in the industry, ensuring that tableware is stylish yet classic, representing the ultimate in taste and design quality. Technological innovation, research and development have been vital elements, resulting in the introduction in 1960 of the first new ceramic body in 200 years. The company is thus the world's leading fine china manufacturer and distributor with an unsurpassed product range.

ABOVE: Examples of Art Director Charles Noke's varied modelling skills.

Royal Doulton
Dickens Ware.

LEFT: A catalogue page showing Royal Doulton 'Dickens Ware', first introduced in c.1908.

FAR LEFT: The 'Dante Vase', modelled by Charles Noke with painted panels by George White, exhibited at Chicago in 1893.

THE FIRST BONE CHINA IN SPACE

In the Sir Henry Doulton Gallery is one of three unique plates which have all orbited the world 92 times. The three plates were carried on the space shuttle *Discovery* in 1984. *Discovery* was named after Captain Scott's famous ship that sailed to the Antarctic in 1905, and which was supplied with a full service of Royal Doulton tableware. It was thus only appropriate that Royal Doulton china should accompany the astronauts, thus becoming the first bone china in space. The second and third examples of the plate are now in the Smithsonian Museum in America and on Captain Scott's ship in Dundee.

ROYAL RECOGNITION

1885   Henry Doulton was awarded the Albert Medal of the Royal Society of Arts. The Prince of Wales actually visited the Royal Doulton factory in Lambeth to present this award in front of the whole workforce. Previous recipients include Sir Rowland Hill, creator of the Penny Black, and Louis Pasteur.

1886   Henry Doulton was appointed Potter to the Prince of Wales.

1887   Queen Victoria knighted Henry Doulton, making him the first potter ever to receive this award.

1901   King Edward VII put the Royal in Royal Doulton when he conferred the honour of a Royal Warrant on the company and at the same time granted the company the specific right to use the title 'Royal'. The Royal Warrant of Appointment has been held to successive monarchs ever since.

1966   Royal Doulton was presented with one of the first Queen's Awards, granted for technological achievement.

1970   Royal Doulton was given the Queen's Award for outstanding export performance.

INTERNATIONAL RECOGNITION

Since the Great Exhibition of 1851, Royal Doulton has exhibited throughout the world. Listed below are some of the many exhibitions where the company received awards and honours.

1851   London – Great Exhibition. Each of the Doulton exhibits gained a silver medal

1862   London

1867   Paris

1876   Philadelphia – 5 first-class awards
Following the Philadelphia Exhibition in 1876, a selection of Doulton art wares was among a range of British ceramics presented to the Meiji emperor in Japan by Dr Christopher Dresser, the eminent Victorian designer. These pieces are now housed in the National Museum of Tokyo.

1878   Paris – Henry Doulton presented with Chevalier d'Honneur Grand Prix

1886   Liverpool

1887   Manchester

1888   Glasgow

1893   Chicago

1904   St Louis, USA

1925   London

1958   Brussels; EXPO Japan

1986   National Garden Festival

1992   EXPO Seville – 'Discovery', the largest figure ever made by Royal Doulton, was exhibited

FIGURES

The Royal Doulton Figure Collection is housed in the Visitor Centre, where there are nearly 1,500 figures on show. The collection includes early examples of Royal Doulton's modellers' skills, rare and unusual pieces, and more recent and current designs.

Although George Tinworth was the first artist in the company to model figures, his work was mainly of small animals or of a religious nature. It was Charles Noke's idea to revive the Staffordshire tradition of modelling that led to the original Royal Doulton figures. Noke, who came to Royal Doulton in 1889 and was Art Director from 1914, recruited a team of modellers to create figures to represent historical and fantasy figures as well as literary characters.

Among Noke's team of craftsmen was Leslie Harradine, who went on to become one of the company's most prolific modellers. Some of his figures, dating back to 1921, are still popular with collectors to this day. Among them are the discontinued 'Sam Weller' (HN 531), 'The Flower Seller's Children' (HN 1324) and the current best known and loved figures 'The Old Balloon Seller' (HN 1315) and 'Top o' the Hill' (HN 1834). As one of the oldest, yet most popular, figures, 'Top o' the Hill', the windswept young lady holding her hat, was chosen as the emblem of the Royal Doulton Visitor Centre. The original idea for the figure came from a calendar design of the 1930s published by Raphael Tuck and Sons Ltd.

With passing years, styles change, and Royal Doulton figures reflect these trends, from the bathing belles and beauties of the 1920s, such as 'The Mirror' (HN 1852) and 'The Bather' (HN 1238) to contemporary designs such as 'Images'. The latter's modern but classic lines, in pure white china (or jet black basalt), clearly show the craftsmanship and exquisite work of the modeller.

Names of figures are often inspired by a detail in the composition or in recognition of someone. For example,

ABOVE: A selection of Harradine's figures, including 'Nadine' (HN 1885), 'Dulcinea' (HN 1343) and 'Gloria' (HN 1700).

BELOW LEFT: 'The Flower Seller's Children' (HN 1324).

A ROYAL CHRISTENING

Queen Mary christened the first figure while on a visit to the Burslem factory in 1913. She stopped at a figure of a small child in a nightgown modelled by Charles Vyse and said, 'Oh, isn't he a darling'; since then the figure has been known as 'Darling'. Figures have also been referenced with an HN number, after Harry Nixon, who was the first manager of the figure-painting department. 'Darling' was referenced HN 1, and all subsequent models have a different HN number.

LEFT: *A group of figures from the 'Images' collection: 'Wedding Day' (HN 2748) by Doug Tootle, 'Over the Threshold' (HN 3274) by Robert Tabbenor and 'Happy Anniversary' (HN 3254) by Doug Tootle.*

LEFT: *Two Harradine figures inspired by contemporary fashion illustrations – 'Contentment' (HN 421) and 'Lady With Shawl' (HN 447).*

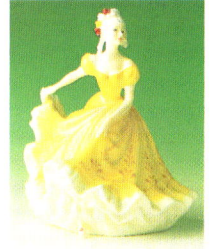

ABOVE: *'Ninette' (HN 2379) by Peggy Davies, first issued in 1971.*

'Ninette', a figure with a daintily pointed toe and swirling skirt, was named after the ballet dancer Ninette de Valois, and the figure 'Just For You' depicts a young girl giving a flower to a grown-up lady. Research is also carried out to find the most popular Christian names of 21, 40 and 50 years ago. These names are given to figures so that they may be appropriate to people celebrating 21st birthdays, or 40th and 50th anniversaries.

Within the last half-century, Royal Doulton has produced the work of a number of great modellers, such as Margaret May Davies, better known to her hundreds of followers as Peggy Davies. She worked for the company from 1939 until she retired in 1984. Mary Nicoll, Eric Griffiths, Bill Harper, Robert Tabbenor, Peter Gee, Alan Maslankowski, Nada Pedley, Pauline Parsons, Valerie Annand, Doug Tootle and Tim Potts are also artists who have contributed to the great success of the figure collections.

RIGHT: *'Sunshine Girl' (HN 1344) by Leslie Harradine, 1929 to c.1938.*

FIGURES

PRESTIGE AND LIMITED EDITION FIGURES

It is the Prestige figures that show the full glory of the Royal Doulton craft skills. 'Princess Badoura' (HN 2081) is 20 inches (50.5 cm) tall, and was first cast in 1952. Inspired by the story from *The Arabian Nights*, 'Princess Badoura' takes several months to make, because the figure has to be fired six times and the hand painting alone takes over 160 hours to complete.

'The Charge of the Light Brigade' (HN 3718) is an exceptional figure, capturing the moment when the British Light Brigade of Cavalry was ordered to charge against Russian positions in the Crimean war. The fear and despondency of both Lancer and horse in full flight have been skilfully portrayed by the modeller. The sculpture was extensively researched to ensure historical accuracy, and took over 18 months to model.

To celebrate the centenary of Sir Henry Doulton's death in 1897, a magnificent model depicting Henry V at Agincourt has been created. As with all the other Prestige figures, 'Henry V at Agincourt' is exclusively available to order by special commission.

There are also special limited edition figures. These are often themed groups of figures which are introduced at regular intervals over several years. Each figure in a limited edition is clearly marked with the total size of the edition run and the number within the edition that the figure represents.

Limited edition figures are highly detailed models and are often representative of a specific historical period, or portray a real-life character. Costume details are extremely important, and accessories such as musical instruments or sporting equipment are often used to complement each figure.

ABOVE LEFT: 'Anna of the Five Towns' (HN 3865) by Tim Potts, a figure inspired by the Arnold Bennett novel of the same name. The figure is only available at the Visitor Centre.

ABOVE RIGHT: 'The Charge of the Light Brigade' (HN 3718) by Alan Maslankowski.

OPPOSITE: The Prestige figure 'Princess Badoura' (HN 2081).

FIGURES

RIGHT: 'Amy' (HN 3316) by Peter Gee, the first Figure of the Year, was produced only in 1980.

ABOVE: Figures of Henry VIII and his six wives, a limited edition series introduced in 1991.

Some figures, such as Figure of the Year and Collectors' Club exclusive figures, are only produced for one year. Introduced in 1980, 'Amy' (HN 3316) was the very first Figure of the Year, and she has since become very popular with collectors. So if you are at a loss as to what to collect from among the huge variety that Royal Doulton has to offer, the annual figures (and Character Jugs) provide a good basis on which to build, and you know that each piece will only be made in the year in question.

Since 1984 a special edition 'Pretty Lady' has accompanied Michael Doulton on his national and worldwide tours. Michael Doulton is the great-great-great-grandson of John Doulton, founder of Royal Doulton, and as President of the International Collectors' Club he travels the world, meeting collectors. His special figure is only produced for a year and is only available when Michael is visiting a store in person. Many collectors ask him to autograph the base of the figure and this is a task he is delighted to undertake.

CANCARA'S STORY

Another traditional area of design at Royal Doulton is animal modelling. This is mainly carried out at the John Beswick Studios in Gold Street, Longton, where the animals are also produced. The black horse Cancara is the symbol of Lloyds Bank. Sculptor Graham Tongue took over 18 months to perfect the model and solve the technical problems of the pose which portrayed Cancara rearing up. As with all models of real animals, Graham visited the horse and examined it carefully from many angles, taking photographs and getting to understand its character. All this information was then interpreted by Graham as he created the sculpture. The skills and knowledge of the Beswick factory team – the mould-makers, kiln-placers, casters and decorators – were then used in creating production models from the original clay. The model of Cancara has been presented at the BAFTA Ceremony in recent years to the winner of the Lloyds Bank People's Film Award. The first recipient was film director Steven Spielberg for Jurassic Park.

CHARACTER JUGS

TOBY GILLETTE

In 1984, schoolboy Toby Gillette wrote to the popular BBC TV programme *Jim'll Fix It*, to ask if Jimmy Savile could fix it for him to have a Toby Jug made in his likeness because of his name. Typically Toby Jugs depict old men, but Royal Doulton was happy to take on this challenge. The company produced three Jugs. One was given to Toby, one was retained for the Sir Henry Doulton Gallery and the third was auctioned for charity, raising over £15,000.

The early Lambeth pieces helped to inspire Charles Noke to introduce, in 1934, a range of Character and Toby Jugs. Continuing the 18th-century Staffordshire tradition of Toby Jug manufacture, skilled modellers created their own distinctive styles to portray characters, both fictional and real. In 1936, the huntsman John Peel became the first famous face in the range. Today, Character and Toby Jugs are made at Royal Doulton's Beswick Studio in Longton, Stoke-on-Trent.

The list of famous people immortalised in ceramics is almost endless. Favourite authors, actors from the stage and screen, classical musicians and pop stars, scientists and sporting heroes – the great and the good – all have found a place in Royal Doulton's hall of fame.

ABOVE: 'The Beatles' Character Jugs were designed by Stan Taylor and produced from 1984 to 1991.

RIGHT: 'John Barleycorn', the first Royal Doulton Character Jug, was modelled by Charles Noke and produced in three sizes from 1934 to 1960. It is intended to be the personification of barley from which malt liquor is made.

NURSERYWARE

Royal Doulton's devotion to the world of children and the nursery dates back to the 19th century, when large, hand painted tile panels depicting scenes from nursery rhymes and fairy tales were produced to decorate the walls of children's wards in hospitals throughout the world, including ones in the cities of London (England), Poona (India) and Wellington (New Zealand).

During the first quarter of the 20th century, production at Burslem included ranges of nurserywares based on themes from literature such as Lewis Carroll's *Alice in Wonderland*, and the popular illustrations of artists like Walter Savage Cooper and Kate Greenway.

ABOVE: Wall plates from Royal Doulton's 'Winnie the Pooh' nurseryware range, introduced in 1996.

ABOVE: Pieces from the 'Nursery Rhymes' and 'Alice in Wonderland' ranges of nurserywares, both issued in the early years of the 20th century.

RIGHT: Figures depicting Winnie the Pooh (right) and his friends Kanga and Roo (left) and Christopher Robin (centre), characters from the popular children's books written by A.A. Milne and delightfully illustrated by Ernest Shepard.

BUNNYKINS

Bunnykins is Royal Doulton's unique character, originally drawn by a nun, Barbara Vernon, who was the daughter of Cuthbert Bailey, general manager of Royal Doulton from 1925. The delightful adventures of Bunnykins and his friends have charmed children for more than 60 years, and this range is the world's most popular bone china nursery-ware. Generations of children from Sydney to Stockholm in ordinary homes and in royal nurseries have enjoyed Bunnykins. Indeed, at this very moment, somewhere in the world, a child is sitting down to enjoy a meal with Bunnykins and his friends.

In 1939, the characters were given life when Charles Noke designed figures and a modelled tea-set. More recently, figures reflecting all aspects of contemporary life from pop music to space travel have been produced by our designers, modellers and decorators at the Beswick factory and these are now a highly collectable part of the Bunnykins series.

BELOW LEFT: A Bunnykins design first issued in 1934.

ABOVE: The first Bunnykins figures by Charles Noke.

BELOW: Pieces made for the 1985 visit of Princess Diana.

ROYAL DOULTON
VISITOR CENTRE
Home of the Royal Doulton Figure

The Royal Doulton Visitor Centre was opened in May 1996 and combines museum displays, a restaurant, cinema and demonstrators' studios with the opportunity to visit the working factory. The Centre is set at the heart of the Royal Doulton factory in Burslem, Stoke-on-Trent, and visitors walk through original factory buildings which have had a variety of different uses since they were first built at the end of the 19th century.

Royal Doulton has welcomed visitors to the factory over many years, and members of the Royal Family have come from the mid-1890s onwards. One of the most famous visits was in 1913 by King George V and Queen Mary. For this visit, a special display of ceramic manufacture was organised on a raised platform, which was sited where the entrance to the Visitor Centre now is. As Queen Mary christened the figure of a boy in a nightgown 'Darling' during this visit, it is appropriate that the Visitor Centre has in turn been christened the 'Home of The Royal Doulton Figure' and the Company collection of figures is on permanent display. Photographs of visitors from the worlds of theatre, television, music and politics are one of the features in the Sir Henry Doulton Gallery.

Royal Doulton itself is close to the centre of the small market town of Burslem, made world-famous by Arnold

TOP: A display in the Royal Doulton Visitor Centre.

ABOVE: The visit in 1913 of George V and Queen Mary.